7 STEPS TO A SUCCESSFUL MARRIAGE

Raul Ries

PUBLISHING
WWW.SOMEBODYLOVESYOU.COM

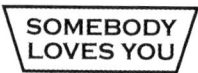

Seven Steps to a Successful Marriage

Raul A. Ries
First Printing © 1997
Revised edition © 2008
Revised edition © 2021 by Somebody Loves You Publishing

Cover Design: Donna McCartney

Requests for information should be addressed to:
Somebody Loves You Publishing
22324 Golden Springs Drive
Diamond Bar, CA 91765-2449
(800) 634-9165
mail@somebodylovesyou.com
www.somebodylovesyou.com

Library of Congress Cataloging-in-Publication Data
Library of Congress Control Number: 2008929637
Ries, Raul
Seven Steps to a Successful Marriage

ISBN: 978-1-934820-05-6
1. Ries, Raul Andrew 2. Calvary Chapel—USA 3. Somebody Love You Radio—USA 4. Evangelist 5. Marriage 6. Family 7. Christian Living 8. Singles

---

All Scripture quotations, unless otherwise indicated, are taken from the Holy Bible: New King James Version, copyright © 1979, 1980, 1982 by Thomas Nelson, Inc. Used by permission.

All rights reserved. No part of this publication may be reproduced, stored in a retrieval system, or transmitted in any form or by any means—electronic, mechanical, photocopy, recording, or any other—except for brief quotations in printed reviews, any form without the written permission of the publisher.

Words or phrases in brackets are not part of the original text. They have been added for clarification.

Printed in the United States of America

CONTENTS

A Word from Pastor Raul 4

CHAPTER 1—WHAT IS MARRIAGE? 7
Designed by God 7
Two Become One 8
An Intimate Bond 9
Prescription for a Successful Marriage 10

CHAPTER 2—SEVEN STEPS FOR HUSBANDS 11
Step #1—Love Your Wife as Christ Loved the Church 11
Step #2—Live with Her for Life 13
Step #3—Be Faithful and Trustworthy to Your Wife 15
Step #4—Be Sexually Satisfied with Your Wife 17
Step #5—Instruct Your Wife in the Word of God 20
Step #6—Honor Your Wife 21
Step #7—Provide for Your Home 23
A Final Note to Husbands 24

CHAPTER 3—SEVEN STEPS FOR WIVES 27
Steps #1—Be Submissive to Your Husband 27
Steps #2—Respect Your Husband 30
Steps #3—Learn from Your Husband 32
Steps #4—Love Your Husband 33
Steps #5—Be Obedient to Your Husband in the Lord 35
Steps #6—Trust Your Husband—and Be Trustworthy 38
Steps #7—Satisfy Your Husband Sexually 40
A Final Note to Wives 42

Conclusion 44

Scriptures to Encourage Husbands and Wives 46

A Word from Pastor Raul

Marriage is not easy. Sharon and I have been married for more than 52 years, and far from being experts, we find ourselves still learning about each other, understanding our differences, denying our selfish desires and picking up our crosses each day.

No, marriage is not easy, but we have found that marriage is a blessing of God. There is no other relationship in which you can experience the joy and intimacy between two human beings as you can in marriage. Though at times it can be hard work, marriage is rewarding and fulfilling.

That is something you do not hear in today's society. In fact, the world takes great lengths in ridiculing and dismissing the God ordained institution of marriage. They replace the love and intimacy found only in marriage with fantasy stories of adulterous affairs, promiscuous sex, couples living together and pornography.

Unfortunately, not only has the secular world bought into these deceptive images, but Christians within the church have as well. According to a study done by Barna Research Group, 33% of the adult population has experienced divorce. Sadly, the divorce rate among born again Christians is 32%.

That is the reason I wrote this book. It is important for Christians in the church, who are already married or desiring to get married, to understand that marriage is a lifetime commitment—one filled with joy, fulfillment, love and reward.

There are many books written on the subject of marriage, but there is only one way to have a good marriage—through Jesus Christ!

Today, many books on the shelves give lip service to biblical commands, because they focus on psychology and humanism. Some books do focus on biblical marriage, but are not easy to read, so they remain on the nightstand, unread.

This book was written around seven biblical principles and commands, directed towards men and women in their marriage relationships. There is no psychology or humanism—just the BIBLE! It is written in a very easy and practical way, so you can not only read through it in its entirety, but refer back to it continually, especially when you may be struggling with an issue in your marriage.

I encourage you to read through the biblical principles and study the Scriptures. As I said, this book was written for men and women—married or single! Besides reading this book, my prayer is that you will put these biblical principles to work in your own life!

You and your marriage MUST be centered on Jesus Christ! Make the commitment to follow the Lord and be obedient to His Word and you will see a difference in your marriage!

Souls for Christ,

Raul Ries

CHAPTER 1

WHAT IS MARRIAGE?

DESIGNED BY GOD

*And the L*ORD *God said, "It is not good that man should be alone; I will make him a helper comparable to him."*

GENESIS 2:18

God created marriage. His plan and purpose is one of fulfillment, completion and satisfaction. In Genesis 2:18, God saw the need in Adam's life for a partner. He needed someone comparable to himself. Notice, God did not say, "I am going to make a slave to serve you." No, right from the beginning, God made woman to be a team member, a partner together with man in marriage.

In Genesis 2:22, it states, *Then the rib which the* L*ORD God had taken from man He made into a woman, and He brought her to the man.* In the Hebrew language, the word *rib* is translated to mean, "curved" [of the body or person]. Woman was created from the closest part to man's heart. He did not create woman from the top of man's head or from the bottom of man's feet, but He made her equal with man—comparable. The LORD designed a perfect relationship, one in which the woman was to be close to the man's heart and the man was to love and protect her continually.

TWO BECOME ONE

God designed marriage to bring a male and female together as one. In Genesis 2:24, it states, *Therefore a man shall leave his father and mother and be joined to his wife, and they shall become one flesh.* The word *joined* literally means "to be glued, to cleave or adhere." When a couple gets married, it is a holy occasion as they are joined before God—the glue being the Holy Spirit. God takes an active role in marriage. He is the center of the relationship, as both the husband and wife walk together in fellowship, seeking God's will.

In 2 Corinthians 6:14, we are reminded, *Do not be unequally yoked together with unbelievers. For what fellowship has righteousness with lawlessness? And what communion has light with darkness?* God forbids a male and a female to be joined together, unless both are in the light, walking in Christ; otherwise, they are out of the will of God.

Now, this does not mean that if you are currently married to an unbeliever, you should get divorced. In fact, Scripture tells us the opposite in 1 Corinthians 7:12-14:

> *If any brother has a wife who does not believe, and she is willing to live with him, let him not divorce her. And a woman who has a husband, who does not believe, if he is willing to live with her, let her not divorce him. For the unbelieving husband is sanctified by the wife, and the unbelieving wife is sanctified by the husband.*

WHAT IS MARRIAGE?

Billy Graham advises:

> The home only fulfills its true purpose when it is God-controlled. Leave Jesus Christ out of your home and it loses its meaning. But take Christ into your heart and the life of your family, and He will transform your home.

AN INTIMATE BOND

Marriage is an intimate bond between a man and a woman. In Deuteronomy 24:5, when a man got married, he was not to go to war or be charged with any business for his first year of marriage. He was to stay home and form a bond with his wife that would make them inseparable throughout their lifetime. The intimacy God designed in marriage is built on Christ, being obedient to His Word and loving one another as He commands. Intimacy includes sexual love, friendship, companionship and trust. You are partners in life and, though you can be opposed in your likes and dislikes, you come together in unity under the Lord.

The Lord often uses the design of marriage as an analogy of our relationship to Christ. Just as the Lord loves us, regardless of our actions, we should love each other, in marriage. When you go into marriage, you need to have your eyes wide open; but when you are married, you need to have them half shut! First Peter 4:8 tells us, *"love will cover a multitude of sins."* In other words, we need to overlook each other's offenses and reach a compromise, considering the good of the other person, rather than ourselves.

Last, marriage is a permanent bond. It is not just for six months, one year, ten years or twenty years; it is "until death do us part." In Matthew 19:6 Jesus said, *"So then, they are no longer two but one flesh. Therefore what God has joined* [glued] *together, let not man separate."*

PRESCRIPTION FOR A SUCESSFUL MARRIAGE

The next two chapters give seven steps for a man and seven steps for a woman to have a successful marriage. These steps come directly from God's Word. I encourage you—whether you are married, engaged or single—to read through the steps and commit to making them a part of your life. If you are married, then put the steps into practice and see how the Lord will revive, repair and rejuvenate your marriage.

The Bible has a great deal to say about marriage. It is never easy to bring two different people, with differing personalities, emotions and thought patterns, together. Marriage takes work—sometimes *hard* work, but there are great rewards in married life. God's Word gives considerable insight into what it takes to make a marriage work. Following is a list of seven duties the Bible describes as the role of the husband. By reading, studying and most importantly *doing* the following steps, you will find your marriage enriched, satisfying and complete—just as God designed it.

Remember, marriage was designed by God to be fruitful, intimate, successful and permanent.

CHAPTER 2

SEVEN STEPS FOR HUSBANDS

STEP #1
LOVE YOUR WIFE AS CHRIST LOVED THE CHURCH

Husbands, love your wives, just as Christ also loved the church and gave Himself for her...

EPHESIANS 5:25

Christ loved the Church sacrificially, even to the point of dying for her. That is the example husbands are to emulate toward their wives. You are to love your wife sacrificially, which means you are to die to yourself. You need to die to your rights, time, pleasures, work and friends—giving yourself to your wife in love. When you love your wife in this way, she is able to yield to you as head of the home—another biblical command.

What does being the head of the home entail? Does it mean that your wife is your personal slave? No! Loving your wife in a godly manner means you are a servant and, with a spirit of servanthood, you are to lead your wife. As head of the home, you are called to lead your wife in prayer, in the Word, in the home, be her protector and be sensitive to her feelings and needs.

You can only love your wife in this way as you are submissive to the Lord. When you put God first in your life and have a committed relationship to Him, then you will love and care for your wife as Christ loved the Church. Jesus is your example. He did not come to be served, but to serve. In this manner, you are to love your wife. Ephesians 5:33 tells us, *Nevertheless let each one of you in particular so love his own wife as himself, and let the wife see that she respects her husband.*

Paul gives us the definition of godly love in 1 Corinthians 13:4-8:

> *Love suffers long and is kind; love does not envy; love does not parade itself, is not puffed up; does not behave rudely, does not seek its own, is not provoked, thinks no evil; does not rejoice in iniquity, but rejoices in the truth; bears all things, believes all things, hopes all things, endures all things. Love never fails.*

In their book, *Love Is Always Right,* Josh McDowell and Norm Geisler offer this input:

> Love is not an option for the Christian. To love is to cooperate with God's unique design for His human creation and know the fulfillment that results from living God's way. Not to love is to miss the purpose for our existence and know little more than frustration and heartache in our dealings with people. To love is always right; not to love is always wrong.

STEP #2
LIVE WITH HER FOR LIFE

"So then, they are no longer two but one flesh. Therefore what God has joined together, let not man separate."

MATTHEW 19:6

In the Old Testament, we find a situation in which the Jewish males, who had been married for a long time, were becoming distraught by the fact that their wives were getting older. They were divorcing their wives and marrying younger women. God condemned this practice in Malachi 2:14-16:

Because the LORD has been witness between you and the wife of your youth, with whom you have dealt treacherously; yet she is your companion and your wife by covenant. But did He not make them one, having a remnant of the Spirit? And why one? He seeks godly offspring. Therefore take heed to your spirit, and let none deal treacherously with the wife of his youth. "For the LORD God of Israel says that He hates divorce, for it covers one's garment with violence," says the LORD of hosts.

God was speaking to these men concerning the wives of their youth. This was their first marriage, therefore binding before the Lord, but these men had come to the place where they were being unfaithful and divorcing their wives. In the Old Testament, a man could go down to the city gates, where the judges presided, and pick up a bill of divorcement, allowing him to divorce his wife for virtually *any* reason, including such a trivial thing as an ill-prepared meal. Make no mistake, God hates divorce.

In Mark's Gospel, the Pharisees tested Jesus by asking Him if it was lawful for a man to divorce his wife. Thinking they had trapped Jesus, the Pharisees cited that Moses permitted a man to write a certificate of divorce and dismiss her. However, we read in Mark 10:5-9:

> *And Jesus answered and said to them, "Because of the hardness of your heart he wrote you this precept* [command]. *But from the beginning of the creation, God 'made them male and female.' 'For this reason a man shall leave his father and mother and be joined to his wife, and the two shall become one flesh;' so then they are no longer two, but one flesh. Therefore what God has joined together, let not man separate."*

Notice, Jesus referred to passages in the Old Testament. Since the beginning of time, God's design has been for one man and one woman to unite in marriage until death. Your commitment to your wife is for life. The reason people were divorcing in the Old Testament is the same reason today—hardness of heart. A hard heart leads to a hard life. You become bitter, unforgiving and selfish. If you want to be in God's perfect will and have Him bless your marriage, then you, as the husband, need to be submitted to Jesus Christ completely. Be obedient to His Word and He will restore, nurture and bless the marriage of your youth.

STEP #3
BE FAITHFUL AND TRUSTWORTHY TO YOUR WIFE

Husbands, love your wives and do not be bitter toward them.

COLOSSIANS 3:19

Can your wife trust you? Are you faithful to her? She needs to know this by your words and actions. Do not say or do things that make your wife think you are bitter towards her or cause her to doubt your love. Reassure her that you will never walk out on the marriage, always remembering your wedding vows and the commitment you made to each other.

When you get married, there is an exchange of rings. Within Christianity the ring is seen as a symbol of eternity—having no beginning and no end. The gold speaks of the deity of Jesus Christ and the center of the ring is where the husband and wife come together as one in Christ. Family, friends and loved ones are outside of that ring. The marriage is between you, your wife and the Lord. The placement of the ring on her finger is a token of your love to her and a commitment of your faithfulness and trustworthiness—you belong to her and she belongs to you.

Let's return to the situation in Malachi 2:14-16. God condemned the Jewish husbands for their behavior towards their wives. They were attracted to the young, heathen women and no longer desired their wives, because they were getting older and were no longer as enticing as the other women. Not only were they unfaithful to their wives, but to God as well. Malachi 2:14-16 states:

> *Because the LORD has been witness between you and the wife of your youth, with whom you have dealt treacherously…Therefore take heed to your spirit, and let none deal treacherously with the wife of his youth.*

To deal treacherously with your wife is to mistreat her—to be unfaithful and untrustworthy.

In Matthew 5:27-28, Jesus tells us:

> *"You have heard that it was said to those of old, 'You shall not commit adultery.' But I say to you that whoever looks at a woman to lust for her has already committed adultery with her in his heart."*

Besides adultery and lust, mistreatment also includes verbal and physical abuse. The Apostle Paul tells us in Ephesians 5:28-29:

> *So husbands ought to love their own wives as their own bodies; he who loves his wife loves himself. For no one ever hated his own flesh, but nourishes and cherishes it, just as the Lord does the church.*

I like what Alistair Begg has to say regarding faithfulness in marriage, in his book, *Lasting Love*:

> In their commitment to the unity of marriage, the couple promises to be faithful to each other if poverty and disease should come upon them. They vow before God and man to be faithful if they meet a more attractive, a

more intelligent, a more compassionate person. The wife vows to be faithful if her husband loses his high-paying job, his esteem before men, his mental faculties, or his youthful vigor. She commits to him even when he doesn't measure up to the standard God has set for him, even when he does not love her as Christ loves the church. The husband vows to be faithful if his wife loses her beauty, her charm, or her tenderness. His commitment remains steadfast even when she is unsubmissive, disrespectful and unable to manage the household well. Through it all the two remain one flesh.

STEP #4
BE SEXUALLY SATISFIED WITH YOUR WIFE

Let your fountain be blessed, and rejoice with the wife of your youth. As a loving deer and a graceful doe, let her breasts satisfy you at all times; and always be enraptured with her love.

PROVERBS 5:18-19

God gave us the gift of sexual intimacy. He intends for us to enjoy it, but only within the boundaries of marriage, between one husband and one wife, committed exclusively to each other for the rest of their lives. Only within this context is sex as beautiful as God intended it to be. In 2 Samuel 13:1-19, David's son, Amnon, thought he loved his half sister, Tamar. In reality, he had no self-control, sexually. Even though Tamar was willing to marry him, Amnon would not wait. He faked an illness to lure her to his bedroom and then he raped her. Afterwards, he was unsatisfied and began to hate her. It was not what he thought it would be.

Reporting on sexual relations in our country, an online article in the August 2002 edition of *The Good News,* by Noel Horner stated:

> Sometimes couples find sex to be intense and gratifying before they marry but after marriage discover it is not as exciting to them. Once they have devalued their respect for each other through premarital sex before marriage, rarely can they find the same attraction and respect shared by couples who marry without premarital sex.

As a husband, you are always to be enraptured by your wife's love and you need to continually kindle the fire. Notice what the Apostle Paul says in 1 Corinthians 7:3-5, regarding sexual relations in marriage:

> *Let the husband render to his wife the affection due her, and likewise also the wife to her husband. The wife does not have authority over her own body, but the husband does. And likewise the husband does not have authority over his own body, but the wife does. Do not deprive one another except with consent for a time, that you may give*

yourselves to fasting and prayer; and come together again so that Satan does not tempt you because of your lack of self-control.

Paul is saying that the husband's body is not his own and the wife's body is not her own—you each have a right to take pleasure in one another. It is important that you do not deprive each other of sexual relations, as this can lead to disastrous problems and temptations. Sex should never be used as a weapon, nor should it be misused, perverted or used as a means of disrespect.

Hebrews 13:4 clearly tells us, *Marriage is honorable among all, and the bed undefiled; but fornicators and adulterers God will judge.* Many women have confided that their husbands are deeply involved in pornography, resulting in selfish, perverted demands. These same men expect their wives to perform the perverted acts that have been depicted in the videos or magazines. This is wrong!

When a husband demands his wife to do something that is disagreeable to her, he is violating the boundaries of love set forth in the Scriptures. Biblical love *seeks not its own.* Whose satisfaction are you seeking, yours or hers? The Bible says love does what is best for the other person.

The husband and wife must be in complete agreement as to the nature of their sexual activity. If one is not in agreement, the partner needs to respect his or her feelings. God did not create sex to be forced upon a person. He expects the sexual acts between a husband and wife to glorify Him, just as in every other area of their lives.

STEP #5
INSTRUCT YOUR WIFE IN THE WORD OF GOD

For the husband is the head of the wife, as also Christ is head of the church; and He is the Savior of the body ...that He might sanctify and cleanse her with the washing of water by the Word...

EPHESIANS 5:23, 26

The husband is to be the spiritual leader of his home. You are called to lead your wife in prayer, in the Word, have family devotions and instigate involvement in your local church. As you draw near to the Lord, in your personal commitment, He will give you the resources to lead your wife and family before Him. There are many good devotionals and study guides available at Christian bookstores and on social media. I recommend you invest in solid reading material that will draw you and your wife into the Word of God.

It has often been said that the family that prays together stays together. Though it is a cliché, there is a great deal of truth in that statement. Consistency in prayer, in the Word and in fellowship, will do much to strengthen your marriage and help you both through the rough times of life.

Keeping Christ in the center of your marriage is *vital*. The role of spiritual leader is important, necessary and rewarding.

STEP #6
HONOR YOUR WIFE

Husbands, likewise, dwell with them with understanding, giving honor to the wife, as to the weaker vessel, and as being heirs together of the grace of life, that your prayers may not be hindered.

1 PETER 3:7

The Lord is calling husbands to be understanding and compassionate towards their wives. Your treatment of her should be defined by gentleness and honor. God has entrusted you with your wife, so she should be given attention, care and respect. Chuck Swindoll, in his book, *Hope Again,* comments:

> God's goal for us as husbands is to be sensitive rather than to prove how strong and macho we are. We need to love our wives, listen to them, adapt to their needs. We need to say no to more and more in our work so we can say yes to more and more in our homes...

There should be no doubt in your wife's mind whether or not you value her opinions and concerns. Some men, however, disregard their wives' input with anger and bitterness, rather than understanding and honor. Read through 1 Peter 3:7 a few times. Do you notice the importance God puts upon honoring your wife? The Scripture clearly teaches that if you DO NOT honor her, your prayers will not be answered!

Peter calls the wife the weaker vessel, not the weak vessel. The Apostle establishes the fact of human frailty in both men and women in 1 Peter 1:24-25, *"All flesh is as grass, and all the glory of man as the flower of the grass. The grass withers, and its flower falls away, but the word of the Lord endures forever."*

More than likely, Peter is referring to the wife as the weaker vessel in a physical sense. Sadly, we live in an age that prefers to eliminate any gender identification and make everything unisex—not male or female. However, God designed men and women as two different individuals with strengths and weaknesses, so they may complement each other.

As a Christian husband, it is important to remember that you not only relate to your wife on an earthly, physical level, but on a spiritual level as well, *…being heirs together of the grace of life* (1 Peter 3:7). Though she is your wife, she is also your sister in Christ. This is important to remember. Your marriage bond always comes back to Jesus Christ.

STEP #7
PROVIDE FOR YOUR HOME

But if anyone does not provide for his own, and especially for those of his household, he has denied the faith and is worse than an unbeliever.

1 TIMOTHY 5:8

Husbands are to be the providers of their homes. God has built into the husband a need to work, as well as provide, and the male often connects his worth with his ability to meet the needs of his family. They are not required to provide an extravagant lifestyle, but they are required to provide for the basic needs of their family. God will honor and bless their hard work.

Today, there are few homes where the man is the sole provider. In most homes both husband and wife work. Some of this is due to necessity, while others are trying to accommodate a certain lifestyle. According to the Department of Labor, in 2016, 71.5% of mothers were in the labor force and 57.8% of them had children under the age of one year.

In marriages with children, it is best for the wife to stay home and take care of the children, instilling the values of Scripture and providing the stability and security children need. Whether the wife works outside of the home or not, it is still the responsibility of the husband to provide for the needs of the family.

If you have a good income, but spend yourself into extreme debt, it is the same as not providing for your family. Do all things in moderation, and do not forget to honor the Lord with, and through, your income.

The Apostle Paul has a strong message for husbands who do not take care of their wives and families in 1 Timothy 5:8, *But*

if anyone does not provide for his own, and especially for those of his household, he has denied the faith and is worse than an unbeliever.

If the husband is healthy and able to work, but refuses, and makes his wife go to work instead, he is worse than an unbeliever. This Scripture is not referring to those who are out of work and busy looking for employment, taking odd jobs on the side to help bring in money. No, Paul is referring to husbands who are slothful and lazy, who have chosen to negate their God-given responsibility and duty. They have denied the faith and are worse than infidels!

A FINAL NOTE TO HUSBANDS

Maybe you have read through these steps and are feeling woefully inadequate or fear you will never be the husband God intended. It is important to remember that you cannot be a godly husband in your own strength and abilities. Just as in our Christian walk, we cannot live as Christian husbands on our own. We need to be in close communion with the Lord and filled with His Holy Spirit in order to walk in Christ's ways. Ephesians 5:18 reminds us, *And do not be drunk with wine, in which is dissipation; but be filled with the Spirit...*

Billy Graham comments:

> Complete fulfillment in marriage can never be realized outside the life in Christ. It is written in the Scriptures that Christ came into the world to destroy the works of the devil. Christ's power over the devil is available to the Christian, and the destroyer of the ideal home can only be routed (put to flight) through the power of Christ.

If we are in a carnal state, it will reflect in our attitudes and behavior towards our wives. Galatians 5:16, 19-21 tells us:

> *I say then: Walk in the Spirit, and you shall not fulfill the lust of the flesh. ... Now the works of the flesh are evident, which are: adultery, fornication, uncleanness, lewdness, idolatry, sorcery, hatred, contentions, jealousies, outbursts of wrath, selfish ambitions, dissensions, heresies, envy, murders, drunkenness, revelries, and the like; of which I tell you beforehand, just as I also told you in time past, that those who practice such things will not inherit the kingdom of God.*

However, if husbands are walking with the Lord and desiring to be godly, God will produce the good fruit desired in the marriage. Galatians 5:22-23 defines the *fruit* well: *But the fruit of the Spirit is love, joy, peace, longsuffering, kindness, goodness, faithfulness, gentleness, self-control. Against such there is no law.*

A right relationship with God will enable husbands to see their wives as gifts from God, making husbands to be more like Christ. When husbands treat their wives as God intended, their wives will respond in love and respect. Not only will their marriage be filled with satisfaction and joy, but God will be glorified in the unity of their walk together.

CHAPTER 3

SEVEN STEPS FOR WIVES

Women have undergone tremendous pressure and confusion regarding their role in marriage. The secular world has taught women that anything less than a career outside of the home is degrading. The role of a wife and mother has been scathed and scorned in the world, leaving Christian women confused regarding the biblical role they are to fulfill. The following seven steps for women are a biblical prescription for a successful, satisfying marriage. They reveal the liberating truth of the Gospel for women and show that their role in marriage is one of freedom, love and partnership.

STEP #1
BE SUMISSIVE TO YOUR HUSBAND

[handwritten annotation: "not sure"]

Wives, submit to your own husbands, as to the Lord.

EPHESIANS 5:22

The word *submit* has received a bad reputation and many women do not even want to use the word. So what does the Bible mean when it speaks of submission?

It is important to look at the verse preceding the directive concerning wives submitting to their husbands. In Ephesians 5:21 we read, *…submitting to one another in the fear of God.* In a godly marriage, both the husband and wife submit to one to another.

The word *submit,* in Greek, means to "be under," just as the husband and wife are under Christ, the wife, in relation to her husband, is placed in a position "under" her husband. Notice, a wife is to submit to her husband, *as to the Lord.* She is not required to submit to sin.

Submission is a voluntary yielding to one's admonition or advice. In this way, marriage calls for both partners to submit to one another, putting the other first. It includes a constant adapting to each other's likes, interests, temperaments, and personality.

So, if the Bible is telling both the husband and wife to submit to one another, why is there a direct command to the wives, specifically, to submit to their husbands?

Consider a women's place in past history and find the answer to this question in the mystery of Christ and His Bride—the Church. The Church submits to Christ.

Contrary to what the secular world advocates, Christianity did much to elevate the status of women and free them from the bondage experienced during Old Testament times.

Under Jewish Law, a woman was merely a possession, having no legal rights whatsoever. A husband could divorce his wife for any reason, but a wife could not leave her husband. In fact, because of this, the woman's father received alimony in advance from the husband-to-be.

In Galatians 3:28, Paul states, *"There is neither Jew nor Greek, there is neither slave nor free, there is neither male nor female, for you are all one in Christ Jesus."* The Bible simply states that there is no difference between man and woman in terms of intelligence, humanness and spiritual matters.

Going forward in this chapter, the Apostle Paul commanded in Ephesians 5:25, *Husbands, love your wives, just as Christ also loved the church and gave Himself for her...* This is a revolutionary statement! That kind of love sets an extremely high standard for husbands to follow. They are to put their wives first, be a servant and love sacrificially.

When the husband was given the directive to love his wife as Christ loves the Church, this was communicating a role of servanthood— sacrificial love. In this context, the wife readily submits herself to husband's loving leadership.

Again, the Bible uses marriage as an illustration of the relationship between Christ and His Church. In 1 Corinthians 11:3 we read, *But I want you to know that the head of every man is Christ, the head of woman is man, and the head of Christ is God.* This Scripture passage gives women the divine example of submission. It states that God the Father is the head of Christ; not in essence or nature, but in function. Christ is in nature God, but He did not retain His privilege. He willingly relinquished it. Jesus humbled Himself and became a Servant.

This relationship example of Christ to God is the same one we find in the structure of marriage. Though the husband and wife are equal in their standing before God, the woman takes the submissive position in relationship to her husband, in order for the family to function in unity. God's design calls for the wife to respect, help and be obedient to her husband, while the husband takes the role of servant leadership towards his wife. Together, both partners submit to the lordship of Christ.

STEP #2
RESPECT YOUR HUSBAND

Nevertheless let each one of you in particular so love his own wife as himself, and let the wife see that she respects her husband.

EPHESIANS 5:33

Do you respect your husband as head of the household? A wife's relationship to her husband mirrors her relationship with the Lord. She cannot submit to her husband if she is not submitting to the Lord. Just as you are to reverence God, you are to reverence (respect) your husband as the provider and head of the home. 1 Peter 3:5-6 tells women:

For in this manner, in former times, the holy women who trusted in God also adorned themselves, being submissive to their own husbands, as Sarah obeyed Abraham, calling him lord, whose daughters you are if you do good and are not afraid with any terror.

When Sarah spoke about Abraham, whether privately or publicly, it was always respectfully, building him up instead of tearing him down. This holds especially true when relating to children. Wives should never put down their husbands in front of their children. What about you? Do you speak lovingly and respectfully of your husband to others? To your children?

Understand, the Bible does not portray Abraham as being perfect. He was not always the best husband, because he made his share of mistakes. Sarah respected him because God put him in a position of authority, as head of the home. Chuck Swindoll, in his book, *Hope Again*, writes:

> The fact that Sarah called her husband her lord (Genesis 18:12) reveals much about their relationship. It shows that she respected him, was attentive to his needs, cooperated with his wishes, and adapted herself to his desires.

The word *respect* means, "to show honor and consideration." In 2 Samuel 6:14-22, David was excited to see the return of the Ark of the Covenant to his people—so excited, in fact, that he danced before the Ark of God and all the people. David's wife, Michal, did not respect his leadership and spoke insultingly to him. She did not honor him as the King of Israel or even the leader of the house.

Michal's behavior resulted in David's instant coldness towards her. From that time forward, there would be no intimacy between them. The result was she had no children to the day of her death. Unfortunately, this all came about because Michal could not show any respect for the husband God placed over her.

Do you honor your husband's God-given position of leadership in the home? Do you show consideration for his diligence in providing for you?

STEP #3
LEARN FROM YOUR HUSBAND

Let your women keep silent in the churches, for they are not permitted to speak; but they are to be submissive, as the law also says. And if they want to learn something, let them ask their own husbands at home...

1 CORINTHIANS 14:34-35

Unfortunately, many people have taken these verses in 1 Corinthians literally that women are never to speak in the church. However, we need to read these verses in context. The Apostle Paul is talking to the Corinthian church and referring to Jewish Synagogue which was set up with the women sitting separately from the men in a divided section. In the Synagogue, as the Rabbi was teaching the Word of God, the women would attempt to ask their husbands what the Rabbi meant, and would end up disrupting the service. This Scripture is not saying that women cannot speak in church, but rather, that the husband should be instructing his wife at home, regarding the Scriptures. The Bible clearly teaches that there is spiritual equality between men and women. Throughout the Scriptures we see women involved in all manner of ministries. They learned in perfect submission from their husbands, and served alongside other men of God (Luke 8:1-3). Priscilla and Aquila who were tent makers partnered together in assisting the Apostle Paul (Acts 18).

It is the function of the husband to be the spiritual leader; to pray, and read the Word of God. He is responsible to God for his family; therefore, he must instruct his family as God directs him. As a wife, be teachable, that you may both grow in the faith together. However if the husband is negligent in being the spiritual head of the home, the wife is to be responsible to have a personal relationship with the Lord, and lead her family spiritually.

[handwritten note: Husband has to be spiritual leader again, what if he isn't?]

STEP #4
LOVE YOUR HUSBAND

...that they [the older women] *admonish the young women to love their husbands...*

TITUS 2:4

There is a song by the popular Christian rock group, dc Talk, called *Luv Is a Verb*—an action. That is exactly how 1 Corinthians 13 describes love. It states that love is patient, kind, not envious, not proud, not rude, not selfish, not irritable, is forgiving and thinks no evil.

Love is a decision that turns into an action. Notice, the Bible never defines love as an ideal or an emotion, but as a deed or an activity. First John 3:18 admonishes us, *My little children, let us not love in word or in tongue, but in deed and in truth.* This verse refers to the will, rather than the emotions. Love is based on obedience to God's Word, not on your feelings or your partner's responses. God did not ask us to *feel* like loving, but commanded us to think, act and speak in a loving manner through the enablement of the Holy Spirit. The Lord reminds us of this enablement in Romans 5:5, *Now hope does not disappoint, because the love of God has been poured out in our hearts by the Holy Spirit who was given to us.*

When the Bible instructs wives to love their husbands, it means to overlook offenses with a forgiving heart. It means to be patient and kind even when your husband is not. First Corinthians 13:5 records that love thinks no evil. In other words, love does not take into account the wrong done!

Josh McDowell and Norm Geisler, in their book, *Love Is Always Right,* state:

> Whether its actions or tokens are received, love continues to give. Whenever you withhold your love because someone ignores it or doesn't appreciate it the way he or she should, you're not loving with the love that comes from God.

A loving wife will build up her husband, not only face to face but to her friends and family, as well. Love realizes the best about the person, not the worst. Finally, love looks out for the best interest of the partner, it is others-centered. The main problem in most marriages is self-centeredness. There is too much of self and not enough giving of self! Marriage is a life of self—denial for both husband and wife.

Remember, the Bible has commanded the husband to love his wife as Christ loved the Church. Both husband and wife are to continually love each other. Love is not dependent on feelings or whether the other partner is doing what they are supposed to do. Love is based on commitment to each other and obedience to Jesus Christ.

When a wife chooses to love her husband rather than being bitter and unforgiving, she will see the Lord's blessings upon her marriage.

STEP #5
BE OBEDIENT TO YOUR HUSBAND IN THE LORD

...the older women ...that they admonish the young women...to be discreet, chaste, homemakers, good, obedient to their own husbands, that the word of God may not be blasphemed.

TITUS 2:5

As a wife you have now learned that loving your husband is seen by your actions and not feelings. After the admonishment for the older women to teach the younger women to love their husbands, they should also teach them to be discreet. The word discreet means "curbing one's desires and impulses, self-controlled or temperate."

A wife is to be *chaste*—pure from carnality, modest. Wives are to be homemakers. Most women love to create a cozy *nest* for their family. A husband after working all day should not have to come home to a neglected household. The Word of God teaches that wives are called to be the keepers of the home and family.

A wife is described as *good*—a benefit to her husband. She is of value and she is a virtuous woman.

A wife is also to be obedient to her husband. Once again we see her submissiveness, as the word obedient uses the same military term used in Ephesians 5:22, "to rank under," as soldiers in an army. The word *obedient* means, "to subject oneself, to obey and to be subject to."

I like what Jay Adams, author and counselor, has to say regarding the wife's role in submission and obedience to her husband, in his book, *Solving Marriage Problems*:

> That means that if a husband's thinking is out of line, his wife's task is to help him correct his thoughts. If his life is out of line, her job is to help him return to God's path. If he simply is perplexed in a decision, she must bring her best reasons to the decision-making process. Help, given respectfully, never conflicts with submission. That is because submission requires her to contribute, to

give what she has to offer. And that is what she must do, always in a spirit of respect and with a willingness to obey even if she may not agree.

Part of submission is obedience—even when you do not agree. As Jay Adams stated in the above quote, the wife is to give her input and wisdom to her husband; but when the final decision is made, she must be obedient to the authority of her husband, whether she agrees with him or not. However, she can pray. This kind of obedience comes by trusting the Lord to be faithful to His Word. The Lord has put your husband in authority, you must trust the Lord in the decision being made by him. God will honor your obedience and use it as a means of strengthening your husband's faith, as well.

Remember, the one time you are not to obey your husband is when he is partaking in sin and asking you to participate in something sinful. In these circumstances, you are to obey God, rather than your husband, as stated in Acts 5:29, *"We ought to obey God rather than men."*

If you are putting your faith and trust in God, He will work in your home and bless your family. Believe that God is going to work in your home. The Scripture declares that even if your spouse is not a believer, God will bless your home. First Corinthians 7:14, *For the unbelieving husband is sanctified by the wife, and the unbelieving wife is sanctified by the husband; otherwise your children would be unclean, but now they are holy.* The word *sanctified* means "to make holy" or "set apart."

Regarding this verse, Pastor Chuck Smith said in his commentary, ...so either the husband or the wife believing, brings into the home a holy environment by which the children are covered.

When a wife learns these valuable lessons, she becomes a crown to her husband, a good wife, and the husband knows that he is loved, obeyed and cared for through all of her actions.

STEP #6
TRUST YOUR HUSBAND—BE TRUSTWORTHY

The heart of her husband safely trusts her; so he will have no lack of gain. She does him good and not evil all the days of her life.

PROVERBS 31:11-12

Going back to the book of Genesis, God made Adam and Eve comparable to one another, so they could help each other. In so many marriages, couples are battling each other, rather than supporting and helping one another. In describing a virtuous woman—a woman who fears the Lord, the Proverb simply states that a husband can trust his wife, because she will help him, not hinder him. It also gives great esteem to the role of the wife, as she greatly enriches her husband's life.

SEVEN STEPS FOR WIVES

Trust is fundamental to marriage. Why? Simply speaking, to trust someone means that you have a firm belief in their honesty, integrity and reliability. That is not to say we will never let someone down. We are human and with that comes failure. However, we need to think the best of our Christian mate and have a foundation of trust in our partner. Without the foundation of trust, our marriages will be ruled by bitterness, fear, jealousy and envy, rather than the love that Christ commands.

When trust in a relationship has been betrayed, it shakes and could even destroy the foundation of trust. However, even in this situation, with the Lord's help and guidance, trust can once again be built and a marriage repaired.

In Genesis 12:1-5, Abraham trusted that Sarah would follow him wherever God sent him. Sarah also trusted Abraham. Even though she did not know where they were going or when they would get there. She trusted that he had been directed by God to leave home and go to this new land. It would not be an easy trip because they would be alone, without the support of family and friends. Their house would be a tent, but, in the midst difficult circumstances, Sarah showed a tremendous a~ trust. God blessed her and the world through them.

Does your husband know you trust him? Can your husband trust you? Do you help your husband in his efforts or do you hinder him?

As a wife, you need to encourage your husband in efforts he undertakes as head of the household, and spiritual leader. Share your concerns with your husband on matters where there may be disagreement or conflict. As you offer input and evaluation, devote the matter to prayer, trusting the final outcome to the Lord. In Proverbs 3:5-6, we see God's promise when we trust in Him, *Trust in the* LORD *with all your heart, and lean not on your own understanding; in all your ways acknowledge Him, and He shall direct your paths.*

By encouraging your husband and helping him in the tasks presented to him, you help nurture love and trust in your marriage relationship.

STEP #7
SATISFY YOUR HUSBAND SEXUALLY

Let the husband render to his wife the affection due her, and likewise also the wife to her husband. The wife does not have authority over her own body, but the husband does. And likewise the husband does not have authority over his own body, but the wife does. Do not deprive one another except with consent for a time, that you may give yourselves to fasting and prayer; and come together again so that Satan does not tempt you because of your lack of self-control.

1 CORINTHIANS 7:3-5

Sex is not to be used as a weapon when angry or bitter toward your spouse. It should not be withheld as a means of punishment or manipulation. The only time sex is to be withheld is by mutual consent, for a time of fasting and prayer. Even in this situation, the Scriptures warn husbands and wives to come together again in sexual relations, so that Satan cannot drive a wedge in their marriage, due to sexual abstinence.

One of the many reasons the Lord designed marriage was for the physical, intimate bond between a man and a woman. Within marriage, sex is a God-ordained and mutually pleasing activity. Outside of marriage, sexual abstinence is God's method of protective blessing, but within marriage, sexual abstinence opens the door to Satan who will entice a spouse into lustful behavior—adultery.

When a marriage is suffering, the first casualty is often the sexual relationship between the husband and wife. Just as you are to nurture emotional love for your husband, you also need to nurture your sexual love with him. Hebrews 13:4 states, *Marriage is honorable among all, and the bed undefiled; but fornicators and adulterers God will judge.*

Both husband and wife are called to satisfy each other sexually; however, remember, you both must be in agreement as to the nature of your sexual activity.

A FINAL NOTE TO WIVES

Some of you may have just read the above steps and feel encouraged, though lacking in compliance to these biblical commands. You know that this is what you need to work toward and are excited to begin the journey. Other women may have just read this and are saying, "Well, that is good for you to say, but my husband is cruel—no way will I submit to him." Yet, others may be saying, "But my husband is an unbeliever. Do these seven steps apply to me?"

Let's face it. Husbands, like wives, are not perfect. Many of you probably find yourselves in circumstances far from ideal, and cannot imagine fulfilling the steps we just discussed. However, whether you are married to a mean person, an unbeliever or a wonderful, Christ-loving husband, you are to be obedient to God's Word as a Christian woman.

Following God's Word is not contingent upon whether or not your husband does. Maybe that sounds unfair or unrealistic. However, if you are obedient to Christ and seek His help and strength to fulfill His commands, you will be blessed and your marriage honored. The Bible addresses difficult marriage circumstances in 1 Peter 3:l-6,

> *Wives, likewise, be submissive to your own husbands, that even if some do not obey the word, they, without a word, may be won by the conduct of their wives, when they observe your chaste conduct accompanied by fear. Do not let your adornment be merely outward—arranging the hair, wearing gold, or putting on fine apparel—rather let*

it be the hidden person of the heart, with the incorruptible beauty of a gentle and quiet spirit, which is very precious in the sight of God. For in this manner, in former times, the holy women who trusted in God also adorned themselves, being submissive to their own husbands, as Sarah obeyed Abraham, calling him lord, whose daughters you are if you do good and are not afraid with any terror.

You can make an impact upon your husband by how you live, rather than by what you say. Trust the Lord when He says your husband will be influenced by watching your behavior. Witnessing the loving behavior you manifest towards him, your husband can be quietly led to the Lord.

Above all, remember, the best way to influence a man to become a godly husband is to become a godly wife. (See Proverbs 31)

CONCLUSION

Dr. Charles Stanley shares an encouraging story in his book, *The Glorious Journey*:

> The former president of Columbia Bible College, Dr. J. Robertson McQuilken, resigned to care for his wife, Muriel. She has Alzheimer's disease, and her personality and behavior are quite different from those of the girl Dr. McQuilken married. In a moving tribute to his wife, he summed up how she had so faithfully cared for him and the children over the years. He said, "I don't have to take care of Muriel. I get to take care of Muriel" What a visual aid for the family! Sticking with it. Priorities. One man and one woman for life.

The key to marriage is to stay centered in Jesus Christ. It is only through Christ and His Holy Spirit that we can love selflessly, bear with one another patiently, and have an attitude of forgiveness.

The success of your marriage is dependent upon two things:

1) Your commitment to Christ
2) Your commitment to prayer and the Word of God.

If both are in place, you will have a marriage where there is growth rather than stagnation, love rather than hate, forgiveness rather than bitterness, fulfillment rather than dissatisfaction and faith rather than unbelief.

CONCLUSION

Billy Graham wrote:

> The perfect marriage is a uniting of three persons—a man, a woman and God! That is what makes marriage holy. Faith in Christ is the most important of all principles in the building of a happy marriage and a happy home.

May you seek the Lord's help as you consider marriage, revive your marriage, or take the steps to reconcile your marriage. God would have you come together with your mate, not to divorce. In a world where we are seeing a higher divorce rate even within the Christian marriages, why not try to do things God's way? He created marriage and He knows how to make it work. Stay in His Word and DO what He says, because failure to adhere to God's principles for marriage will result in marital problems. Remember, the condition of your marriage is a thermometer of how hot or cold your relationship is with the Lord! Is it time to take your temperature?

SCRIPTURES TO ENCOURAGE HUSBANDS AND WIVES

GOD'S PLAN FOR MARRIAGE

GENESIS 2:18-24

*And the Lord God said, "It is not good that man should be alone; I will make him a helper comparable to him." Out of the ground the L*ORD *God formed every beast of the field and every bird of the air, and brought them to Adam to see what he would call them. And whatever Adam called each living creature, that was its name. So Adam gave names to all cattle, to the birds of the air, and to every beast of the field. But for Adam there was not found a helper comparable to him. And the L*ORD *God caused a deep sleep to fall on Adam, and he slept; and He took one of his ribs, and closed up the flesh in its place. Then the rib which the L*ORD *God had taken from man He made into a woman, and He brought her to the man. And Adam said:*

> *"This is now bone of my bones*
> *And flesh of my flesh;*
> *She shall be called Woman,*
> *Because she was taken out of Man."*

Therefore a man shall leave his father and mother and be joined to his wife, and they shall become one flesh.

SCRIPTURES TO ENCOURAGE HUSBANDS AND WIVES

MARK 10:6

"But from the beginning of the creation, God 'made them male and female.' For this reason a man shall leave his father and mother and be joined to his wife, and the two shall become one flesh;" so then they are no longer two, but one flesh. Therefore what God has joined together, let not man separate."

INSTRUCTIONS FOR BOTH HUSBANDS AND WIVES

PROVERBS 3:5-6

Trust in the LORD with all your heart, and lean not on your own understanding. In all your ways acknowledge Him, and He shall direct your paths.

1 CORINTHIANS 7:3-5

Let the husband render to his wife the affection due her, and likewise also the wife to her husband. The wife does not have authority over her own body, but the husband does. And likewise the husband does not have authority over his own body, but the wife does. Do not deprive one another except with consent for a time, that you may give yourselves to fasting and prayer; and come together again so that Satan does not tempt you because of your lack of self-control.

1 CORINTHIANS 11:3

But I want you to know that the head of every man is Christ, the head of woman is man, and the head of Christ is God.

1 CORINTHIANS 13:4-8

Love suffers long and is kind; love does not envy; love does not parade itself, is not puffed up; does not behave rudely, does not seek its own, is not provoked, thinks no evil; does not rejoice in iniquity, but rejoices in the truth; bears all things, believes all things, hopes all things, endures all things. Love never fails.

2 CORINTHIANS 6:14-16

Do not be unequally yoked together with unbelievers. For what fellowship has righteousness with lawlessness? And what communion has light with darkness? And what accord has Christ with Belial? Or what part has a believer with an unbeliever? And what agreement has the temple of God with idols? For you are the temple of the living God. As God has said:

> *"I will dwell in them*
> *And walk among them.*
> *I will be their God,*
> *And they shall be My people."*

SCRIPTURES TO ENCOURAGE HUSBANDS AND WIVES

EPHESIANS 5:21-26

...submitting to one another in the fear of God. Wives, submit to your own husbands, as to the Lord. For the husband is the head of the wife, as also Christ is head of the church; and He is the Savior of the body. Therefore, just as the church is subject to Christ, so let the wives be to their own husbands in everything. Husbands, love your wives, just as Christ also loved the church and gave Himself for her, that He might sanctify and cleanse her with the washing of water by the Word.

EPHESIANS 5:33

Nevertheless let each one of you in particular so love his own wife as himself, and let the wife see that she respects her husband.

HEBREWS 13:4

Marriage is honorable among all, and the bed undefiled; but fornicators and adulterers God will judge.

FOR HUSBANDS

PROVERBS 5:18-19

Let your fountain be blessed, and rejoice with the wife of your youth. As a loving deer and a graceful doe, let her breasts satisfy you at all times; and always be enraptured with her love.

PROVERBS 18:22

He who finds a wife finds a good thing, and obtains favor from the Lord.

MALACHI 2:14-16

…Because the Lord has been witness between you and the wife of your youth, with whom you have dealt treacherously; yet she is your companion and your wife by covenant. But did He not make them one, having a remnant of the Spirit? And why one? He seeks godly offspring. Therefore take heed to your spirit, and let none deal treacherously with the wife of his youth. "For the Lord God of Israel says that He hates divorce, for it covers one's garment with violence," says the Lord of hosts. "Therefore take heed to your spirit, that you do not deal treacherously."

MATTHEW 5:27-28

"You have heard that it was said to those of old, 'You shall not commit adultery.' But I say to you that whoever looks at a woman to lust for her has already committed adultery with her in his heart."

EPHESIANS 5:28-29

So husbands ought to love their own wives as their own bodies; he who loves his wife loves himself. For no one ever hated his own flesh, but nourishes and cherishes it, just as the Lord does the church.

SCRIPTURES TO ENCOURAGE HUSBANDS AND WIVES

COLOSSIANS 3:19

Husbands, love your wives and do not be bitter toward them.

1 PETER 3:7

Husbands, likewise, dwell with them with understanding, giving honor to the wife, as to the weaker vessel, and as being heirs together of the grace of life, that your prayers may not be hindered.

FOR WIVES

PROVERBS 31:11-12

The heart of her husband safely trusts her; so he will have no lack of gain. She does him good and not evil all the days of her life.

ACTS 5:29

But Peter and the other apostles answered and said: "We ought to obey God rather than men."

1 CORINTHIANS 14:34-35

Let your women keep silent in the churches, for they are not permitted to speak; but they are to be submissive, as the law also says. And if they want to learn something, let them ask their own husbands at home…

TITUS 2:3-5

…the older women likewise, that they be reverent in behavior, not slanderers, not given to much wine, teachers of good things—that they admonish the young women to love their husbands, to love their children, to be discreet, chaste, homemakers, good, obedient to their own husbands, that the word of God may not be blasphemed.

1 PETER 3:1-6

Wives, likewise, be submissive to your own husbands, that even if some do not obey the word, they, without a word, may be won by the conduct of their wives, when they observe your chaste conduct accompanied by fear. Do not let your adornment be merely outward—arranging the hair, wearing gold, or putting on fine apparel—rather let it be the hidden person of the heart, with the incorruptible beauty of a gentle and quiet spirit, which is very precious in the sight of God. For in this manner, in former times, the holy women who trusted in God also adorned themselves, being submissive to their own husbands, as Sarah obeyed Abraham, calling him lord, whose daughters you are if you do good and are not afraid with any terror.

DIVORCE

MALACHI 2:16

"For the LORD God of Israel says that He hates divorce, for it covers one's garment with violence," Says the LORD of hosts. "Therefore take heed to your spirit, that you do not deal treacherously."

MATTHEW 5:32

"But I say to you that whoever divorces his wife for any reason except sexual immorality causes her to commit adultery; and whoever marries a woman who is divorced commits adultery."

1 CORINTHIANS 7:12-14

If any brother has a wife who does not believe, and she is willing to live with him, let him not divorce her. And a woman who has a husband who does not believe, if he is willing to live with her, let her not divorce him. For the unbelieving husband is sanctified by the wife, and the unbelieving wife is sanctified by the husband; …But if the unbeliever departs, let him depart; a brother or sister is not under bondage in such cases. But God has called us to peace. For how do you know, O wife, whether you will save your husband? Or how do you know, O husband, whether you will save your wife.

PUBLISHING
WWW.SOMEBODYLOVESYOU.COM

BOOKS

Raul Ries

From Fury to Freedom
From Fury to Freedom***
Man: Natural, Carnal, Spiritual
Impurity: The Naked Truth
Sin: The Root of All Evil
Doctrines: A Simplified Road Map of Biblical Truth
Doctrines: A Simplified Road Map of Biblical Truth***
Servant: The Person God Uses
Victory: Overcoming the Enemy
Seven Steps to a Successful Marriage
Seven Steps to a Successful Marriage***
Raising a Godly Family in an Ungodly World
Somebody Loves You Growth Book**
30 Questions that Deserve Answers**
Understanding God's Compassion**
Living Above Your Circumstances:
  A Study in the Book of Daniel
Hear What the Spirit Is Saying
Marriage: Vowed Inseparable
The Sermons of Sermons: Christ's Sermon on the Mount

Chuck Smith

The Philosophy of Ministry: Calvary Chapel*

Sharon Faith Ries

The Well-Trodden Path
My Husband, My Maker
The Night Cometh: Edmund and Naomi Farrel
Written Bible Studies*

Claire Wren

Crimson

PAMPHLETS (Spanish only)

El Pecado de la Ira
El Pecado de la Envidia
El Pecado de la Impureza
El Pecado de la Soberbia

DVDs

Raul Ries

Fury to Freedom*
Taking the Hill: 2-DVD Package*
A Quiet Hope*
A Venture in Faith: The History and Philosophy of the Calvary Chapel Movement*

*available in Spanish
**booklet
***audio book

FILMS

Shane Ries

The Parisian Incident
Cycle
W 3sixty5
Abraham's Desert

Somebody Loves You Publishing
22324 Golden Springs Drive
Diamond Bar, CA 91765-2449
(800) 634-9165
mail@somebodylovesyou.com
www.somebodylovesyou.com

Somebody Loves You Radio is the teaching ministry of Pastor Raul Ries. Since committing his life to Christ in 1972, Raul has been driven to share the message of God's love, to a lost and dying world, on a 30-minute daily program which is heard worldwide on over 350 stations. It can also be accessed on the *Somebody Loves You* website, mobile app, and podcasts. The vision of *Somebody Loves You* is simple but powerful—to reach the world for Christ.